FOOTBALL
LEGENDS

ALEX OXLADE-CHAMBERLAIN

PAUL STEWART

FOOTBALL LEGENDS

ALEX OXLADE-
CHAMBERLAIN

■SCHOLASTIC

For Jose and Anna.

Published in the UK by Scholastic Children's Books, 2021
Euston House, 24 Eversholt Street, London, NW1 1DB
A division of Scholastic Limited

London ~ New York ~ Toronto ~ Sydney ~ Auckland
Mexico City ~ New Delhi ~ Hong Kong

SCHOLASTIC and associated logos are trademarks and/or
registered trademarks of Scholastic Inc.

Text © Paul Stewart, 2021
Cover illustration © Stanley Chow, 2021

The right of Paul Stewart to be identified as the author
of this work has been asserted by him in accordance with
the Copyright, Designs and Patents Act, 1988.

ISBN 978 1407 19855 2

A CIP catalogue record for this book
is available from the British Library.

Printed and bound by CPI Y

Papers used by Scholastic Children's Books are made

Contents

ENGLAND EXPECTS

Everything was going well for Alex Oxlade-Chamberlain. In August 2017, he signed a £35 million five-year contract to play for Liverpool under manager Jürgen Klopp. Gareth Southgate, the England manager, had brought him back into the England squad. In addition, both managers were playing him in his preferred position: midfield.

Then disaster struck.

It happened in the fifteenth minute of the Reds' Champions League semi-final first leg against Roma, on 24 April 2018. Alex went in for a challenge on Roma's Aleksandar Kolarov – and ended up on the ground, writhing in agony. He had injured his right knee and would play no further part in the Champions League, which Real Madrid went on to win, beating Liverpool 3–1 in the final.

During Alex's surgery eight days later, doctors discovered how badly the ligaments in his knee had been damaged. Rumours appeared in the papers. He would be out of action for three months. Six months. A year. In July, Jürgen Klopp confirmed to reporters that Alex would miss the rest of the 2018–19 season – both national and international matches – to focus on his recovery.

This injury was not his first. Far from it. In October 2012, as an Arsenal player, hip problems had caused him to miss five matches. After that, a series of lower-body injuries kept putting him out of action. The worst occasion was 19 August 2013 when Alex had a nasty collision with Aston Villa defender Antonio Luna. A badly injured knee then meant he missed the next thirty matches, including England's World Cup qualifiers against Moldova and Ukraine.

The injury he got in the Roma match, however, was far more serious. The worst rumours proved correct. It was a full year later – on 26 April 2019 – when Alex finally made his return to the team.

At the time of the injury, Alex used Instagram to explain how he felt. "Absolutely devastated to have picked up this injury at such a crucial time in the season. Gutted I won't be able to play any further part now in our Champions League run for Liverpool, and also the World Cup with England."

Gutted he may have been, but Alex was not only thinking of himself. That is not in his character. Before the match, fighting had broken out when Italian ultras had attacked Liverpool supporters. Fifty-three-year-old fan Sean Cox was taken to hospital with a terrible head injury. Setting aside his own problems, Alex made this comment.

"However, this all pales in comparison to how the family of the Liverpool fan badly hurt before last night's game must be feeling. My thoughts are with him and his loved ones."

It is easy to see why Alex is so popular with the fans.

Following the knee injury, Alex put all his energies into getting match-fit again. As he himself put it, "As a character I'm positive, and I'm trying not to let myself get too down. Obviously I've got a tough rehab ahead of me and moping around isn't going to get me through that!" During his recovery, Alex maintained his upbeat attitude, sharing online with his fans, "It's going well – very boring, very slow, very long! But I'm in good spirits and I'm really positive about it."

It was important for Alex to remain positive and focus on his recovery. If he didn't get better, he would not play again – and that was not an option. It was a setback, that was all. Alex had had setbacks before and overcome them. This is what he would do again. Years earlier, while playing at Arsenal, he said something similar, something that had motivated him throughout his life:

"Me being myself, I'm not happy when I'm not playing."

KICKING OFF

Alexander Mark David Oxlade-Chamberlain was born on 15 August 1993 in Portsmouth, UK. His mother, Wendy Oxlade, was a physiotherapist. His father was professional footballer Mark Chamberlain. On 24 June, five years later, his brother Christian was born. The family was complete.

Alex's grandfather on his father's side had emigrated from Jamaica to England in the late 1950s and settled in Burslem, Stoke-on-Trent. He and his wife had two sons, Neville and Mark. Both of them became professional footballers.

Mark, the younger brother, began his career with Port Vale in 1978. Four years later he went to Stoke City, and from there to Sheffield Wednesday, Portsmouth, Brighton & Hove Albion and Exeter City. He ended his career as a player-manager at Fareham Town from 1997–98.

Mark played for England between 1982 and 1984. He represented his country four times in Under-21 teams, and was capped for England eight times. Playing as a winger or right-back, Mark was well known for his speed. Port Vale coach Graham Barnett called him "a gazelle"; teammate Robbie Earle summed it up like this: "Mark could do it all. Run, pass, shoot, make goals and score them." When Mark and brother Neville were both playing for Port Vale, they would sometimes swap shirts at half-time to confuse the opposition.

With a famous footballer for a father, Alex had someone to look up to – and also to *live* up to. That said, when his father's career was at its best, Alex was very young. As Mark himself remarked, "I think both Alex and his brother look at me a bit dubiously when I tell them I played for England. They just see an old man!"

Pulling a Fast One

From the moment Alex could walk, he was happy kicking a ball. Soon, Mark was taking his young son up to the park near the Port Solent marina for a kickabout. And later, when Alex grew older, for serious football training. Like his father, Alex was quick – though not as quick as he thought he was.

Alex and his dad finished every session with a race. Alex always won – until the day everything changed. "Until I was nine or ten I genuinely thought I was quicker than him," Alex explains. "Then one day, when we raced, he battered me and I didn't know what had happened. I started telling him he was cheating. Obviously, he thought at that age I could take losing."

Mark tells the same incident differently. "It got to the point when he was eleven or so – I can't remember exactly how old – and he was talking to some people who had seen me play. They told him, 'Your Dad's quick,' and he said, 'Quick? He's not quick. I always beat him!' That's when I told him, 'But I let you win.'"

It was one of those childhood events that helped

to form Alex's character. It taught him not to be boastful or over-confident, and it showed him that however good he might be, there was always room for improvement.

Growing up, football was a big part of Alex's life and he spent a lot of time playing and training with his dad. But it wasn't always just the two of them. When he came out of coaching, Mark worked with underprivileged children on a council estate in Southampton. Alex used to go along with his dad and spend time with the children living on the estate – he'd play football and mess about with them, becoming good friends with many of the other kids.

This time spent out in the local community showed Alex how football can bring people from different backgrounds together. The experience had a lasting effect on him and he carried this sense of community and team spirit into his professional career. Even when Alex moved up in the league, from St Mary's to the Emirates Stadium, he never forgot where he came from, or the people who helped him get there. When Alex's former Southampton teammate Adam Lallana met up with him after

Alex's move to Arsenal he tweeted, "Still down to earth as ever."

Mum's the Word

Since Alex followed in his father's footsteps and became a footballer, it is tempting to think that Mark played the more important role in his childhood. This, of course, was not true. His mother Wendy was also a massive influence in Alex's life.

Mark's career was at its peak around the time Alex was born. When Alex was growing up, his father was away on and off playing for his team all over the country. This meant that it often used to be just Alex and his mum at home – until his little brother came along when he was five. Although it was difficult for Alex and his family when Mark was away, it meant Alex became very close to his mum.

Wendy's physiotherapist job was a great help to Alex. She understood how important it was to stay fit and healthy. Wendy was also athletic herself and had once had a trial for the England volleyball team when she was young. She would make sure that Alex was eating the right foods to help him have the energy for all the football training and matches. When Alex was younger, in pre-season Wendy would take him out running and get him to do press-ups to keep his fitness levels high.

However, although both she and her husband were sporty, Wendy also wanted her son to get a good education. Alex was sent to a local independent school, St John's College, Southsea, where he did well. Although the football pitch was where Alex excelled, Wendy encouraged him to do his homework for school to make sure he got good grades. All his work paid off, because when Alex finished secondary school he earned one A*, one A, five Bs and three Cs in his GCSEs. Had he not become a professional footballer, Alex might well have gone to university.

Alex's 'Bottom'

One career that Alex had no intention of pursuing was acting. However, despite being uninterested in it, Alex was rather a good actor, and his teachers often encouraged him to be more involved and take part in school performances. When Alex was ten years old, he was asked to play the role of Bottom in the school's adaptation of William Shakespeare's *A Midsummer Night's Dream*. Alex was expected to act *and* sing.

Performing in front of a crowd is nerve-racking for anyone, but when you've got to sing in front of your entire school then it can be terrifying. One of Alex's main scenes in the play involved Bottom performing for the other characters. The script called for everybody to cover up their ears when Alex (Bottom) had to sing an awful tune. Alex worked with the school's musical director, Sarah Reeves, who taught him to sing as badly as possible.

Dressed in a donkey-head costume, Alex gave it his best shot. The performance terrified him. He didn't want to end up a laughing stock in the school. After all, credibility with your classmates is very important when you are in Year 6. But it all went well. Just like with football and school work, Alex put everything into his performance and it paid off – he was given a standing ovation. It was the kind of experience that would prepare him for being in the spotlight when he was older.

Once again, an incident from Alex's childhood proved important in rounding his character.

His natural reserve had been overcome, and the drama lessons at school helped him to deal with performing in public. Everyone knew that Alex was good at football, but acting really helped build his confidence, which would help him to make the leap from public speaking to playing football in front of thousands of spectators each week.

Looking back on his childhood and the influence of his parents, Alex clearly had a lot of guidance from both his dad and his mum. He always respected their advice and still does as an adult. Growing up with a famous footballer for a father had its difficulties, but it has also been a huge help to Alex and he continues to trust his dad, especially when it comes to football.

Not that he was ever pushed into playing football unwillingly. As Alex himself said, "If I hadn't wanted to become a footballer, Dad wouldn't have made me do it. But from day one I showed him I did want to do it and he did everything to help me along." On occasions, however, this "help" verged on tough love.

For instance, while Mark was at Southampton Academy, and Alex was in the Under-11 team he was coaching, they played away at Tottenham. In the first ten minutes of the game, Alex made two bad mistakes. Mark told him what he'd done wrong and what he needed to do, but Alex didn't listen to his dad so Mark took him off the pitch.

"Sit there! Actually, don't. Go and sit in the car."

Alex was distraught. He had travelled all that way and only been in the match for fifteen minutes. He was in floods of tears.

"You'll listen to me next time," Mark told him.

And he was right.

However strict they were, Alex's parents always wanted him to do the best he could and they both encouraged him in and out of school. It is Mark himself who summed it up best: "I did the football and his mum did the education," he said. "Football won out."

A SPORTING CHANCE

At St John's College, football was offered as a sport –
but only in the juniors. After the age of eleven, it
was rugby in the winter and cricket in the summer.
Any football was limited to kicking a ball around the
playground. By this time, however, Alex was already
playing football regularly at Southampton Academy.

Alex was seven years old when his father first
took him on the hour-long drive from Portsmouth to
Southampton to enlist at the academy. In those early
years, Alex started in the development schemes at
Under-8 level, then he went on a six-week trial. He
was signed for his first contract when he was eight.

From then on, every year he worked his way up to the Under-14s team.

Having identified the youngster's talent, Southampton Academy had taken him on and Alex's football career was underway. However, back at St John's, others had also spotted his sporting potential. For a while it looked as though, if Alex did make it to a premier team, it might not be as a footballer.

A Wealth of Talent

Given the sportiness of both his parents, it is no surprise that Alex grew up as an all-round sportsman. At junior school, he excelled at athletics, particularly sprinting. And later, in the seniors, his talent at both cricket and rugby became obvious. Alex was on a sports scholarship at St John's, so this meant that he had to play rugby for the school team. He usually played scrum-half; sometimes full-back.

Although Alex loved football, others saw his real potential for rugby. He was spotted by a scout from Aviva Premiership side London Irish and invited to go for a trial. Perhaps because he was not particularly tall in his early teens, Alex's own attitude to rugby was a little uncertain and he remembers the struggles he faced during matches. "I was always nippy in rugby, getting away from people in the first five yards, but then they'd catch me up with their big legs." Alex didn't enjoy rugby very much, especially when everyone got bigger and stronger and the game started to get more physical.

In the end, the London Irish scout was told by his teacher that there was no chance of him joining up. Alex wanted to be a footballer. The offers, however, were not over yet. Having taken up cricket, Alex discovered that he not only liked the game but was also very good at it. He played both for the school and South East Hampshire.

Alex was a real all-rounder in cricket – he could bat, keep wicket and bowl. He was so talented at the game that he was offered Hampshire trials as a wicket-keeper and batsman, but he couldn't go to the trials because of football.

Growing Pains

Having turned down the possibility of a rugby or cricketing future, Alex concentrated on his football.

He was doing well at Southampton Academy. They recognized his skill, despite his slight build.

The Under-18 coach, Anthony Limbrick, explained how Southampton Academy selected players and spotted their potential quite young, but not necessarily what other clubs might consider potential. "Some clubs go for the bigger, stronger and more physical players. We are more patient, and give our players more time to develop because we see more ability in them technically."

There came a point, though, when even Southampton were uncertain about Alex's future. He was simply too small. Alex was told he had two months to prove that he deserved his place at the academy. As a backup, his father took him to Fulham Football Club, but Alex failed a trial there. So he went away over the Christmas break and focused on improving. Alex worked really hard – going to the gym more, running and doing other exercises to build his strength and skills – to come back fitter and stronger. His natural football ability helped him, but his hard work paid off. Alex got his scholarship.

Football Academies

Many children display a natural talent for football, but truly great players are created, not born, learning the finer points of the game at football academies all over the world. In the UK, the top five academies are currently considered to be Manchester United, Liverpool, Everton, Aston Villa and Southampton.

Reasons for an academy taking a young player on can vary. When Alex joined St Mary's, many clubs went for the bigger, stronger and more physical players. However, Southampton was more patient, giving their players time to develop when they recognized technical ability.

The Home Stretch

Having trained so hard, Alex was now fit and strong. He had "the upper body build of a middleweight boxer", as Stewart Henderson, one of Southampton's team coaches, recalls.

Even though Alex was one of the smallest players on the team, he tried not to worry too much about his size. "You have to give young players time to grow sometimes," Alex later noted, "because everyone develops at different rates and I was an August baby, so I was the youngest in the year." Like Gareth Bale, another product of Southampton Academy, Alex had been a late developer.

But he'd made it in the end.

Throughout this time of uncertainty, Alex's father Mark came into his own. As a former footballer himself, he knew all about the physical side of the game, but he also understood the importance of a positive attitude. He offered his son lots of encouragement, as well as insisting on discipline. At the time, Alex sometimes found this difficult. "Growing up, it was frustrating not being able to do 'nothing' things that my friends did. Going to the odd party here or there. But my dad always set the record straight. If I wanted to make it, I couldn't do those things at that time."

And Alex *did* want to make it.

In his first season with Southampton Under-18s, he spent most of the time on the bench. But then things changed. "I had one game in the FA Youth Cup, which was a rare start for me," he remembers. "Although we lost 3–1 at QPR, I had a really good game and I was with the first team from then onwards."

On 2 March 2010, Alan Pardew gave him his debut in the first team. Alex was subbed on to the pitch in midfield in a 5–0 victory over Huddersfield. He became the second youngest Southampton debut player, after Theo Walcott five years earlier. Alex was 16 years and 199 days old.

As Pardew himself later commented, "He's an absolutely outstanding player. I gave him his debut at sixteen. I don't give many people debuts at sixteen. He just stood out that he was going to be an amazing player."

Alex's professional career had begun.

AIMING FOR THE STARS

"Every boy has role models," Alex once said, and for him it was Thierry Henry. For years he had idolized the Frenchman's skills on the pitch. "He's a star, isn't he?" he would say. Now Alex was playing professionally for Southampton. It was up to him whether he became a role model for the next generation of players.

On 8 May 2010, in the final match of the season, Southampton played Southend United. Alex came on in the eighty-second minute as a substitute for Jason Puncheon. Southampton had come from behind to win 3–1. It was a good result. But as manager Alan

Pardew noted, "The result was certainly better than the performance."

It was three months later – after a Swiss tour and a series of friendly matches – when Alex and the rest of the team had the chance to perform better.

A Different League

Alex remained on the bench for the first match of the 2010–2011 season, when Southampton lost 1–0 to Plymouth Argyle. But three days later, on 10 August, he made his first competitive start. The game was against AFC Bournemouth in the first round of the Carling Cup, and Southampton won 2–0. Alex scored one of those goals in the eighty-sixth minute. It was his first senior goal. Then, on 20 August 2010, five days after his seventeenth birthday, he signed a three-year contract with Southampton.

Southampton FC

Alex was at Southampton from 2 March 2010 to 8 August 2011. When he started, they were in League One, and he helped their promotion to the Championship for the 2011–2012 season. They are now back in the Premier League. Alex played in one of the new home shirts, unveiled on 10 June 2010 in celebration of the club's 125th anniversary.

The 'firsts' kept coming. On 4 September, Alex saw his first League One start with a 2–0 loss at home to Rochdale. His first league goal – and match winner – came the following month in a 2–1 victory over Oldham Athletic. He scored two more goals and made an assist in a 4–0 win over Dagenham & Redbridge on 2 November, when he was also voted Man of the Match in a league game for the first time.

Alex finished the 2010–2011 season with a total of nine league goals. He was also named in the PFA League One Team of the Year and nominated for the LFE's Football League Apprentice of the Year. He was growing as a player. And although he had signed a contract with Southampton, people were beginning to talk about the possibility of a transfer.

Southampton had just been promoted back to the Championship after two years in League One, but the atmosphere at the club was not very positive. Markus Liebherr, its owner, had died of a heart attack in August. Weeks later, manager Alan Pardew – who had given Alex his first break – was sacked. Because of all this, no one was surprised when, in June, Mark stated that his son was eager to join Premier League club Arsenal.

A Hard Lesson

Alex signed for Arsenal on 8 August 2011. Neither club revealed the money involved in the transfer, but the newspapers suggested that the fee was £12 million, with 'add-ons' pushing the total up to £15 million.

It was looking good. Alex had ended up playing for the team his hero, Thierry Henry, had played for. Alex received a lot of praise from his new teammates, which was an encouraging start to him joining the big league. Robin van Persie was quoted as saying, "I'm sure he has a bright future for Arsenal and England. He has pace, he is clever, knows when to pass, when to keep the ball and has good technique … he has a bit of everything." Arsenal and France full-back Bacary Sagna agreed. "He has the talent to become one of the best players in football."

The relationship between a player and the manager is often crucial to morale and the way a team performs. There have been many infamous clashes over the years. In 2002, Roy Keane publically challenged Ireland manager Mick McCarthy for his lack of preparation. In 2003, the then manager of Manchester United, Sir Alex Ferguson, had a run-in with David Beckham that hit the headlines.

In contrast, after his move to Arsenal, Alex spoke highly of Arsène Wenger . The first time he met him was the day he signed. "He's a nice man, you know?

He's very calm and has that aura about him. You know he's the boss." His new manager was similarly impressed. "We are looking forward to him fulfilling his huge potential with Arsenal."

Later, Alex explained that the manager's words had been inspirational. They gave him a lot of drive to come in and prove that Wenger had made the right decision in signing him up for Arsenal.

Then, on 28 August, his Arsenal debut arrived. Alex became the 150th player to represent Arsenal in the Premier League when, in the sixty-second minute, Arsène Wenger substituted him on for Francis Coquelin. Arsenal was already 3–1 down. Despite a second-half goal from Van Persie, the rot continued. Five more Manchester United goals made the result a disastrous 8–2. For Alex, it could not have been more disappointing. Yet instead of wallowing, he learned from the defeat. "To have that sort of experience so early on in my career, I took a lot away from that."

Less than a month later, on 20 September, Alex scored his first goal for Arsenal. It was in the fifty-eighth minute of a League Cup match against Shrewsbury Town. Then, eight days after that, he scored the opening goal – driving a low shot into the bottom right corner – in the eighth minute of his UEFA Champions League debut against Greek team Olympiacos. Alex was thrilled. "That feeling pushed me," he said. "It made me realize I am capable of it, but I also realized I still had a long way to go."

As the months passed, Alex's game continued to get better. At the end of his first season in the Premier League, he was nominated for PFA Young Player of the Year. He was the youngest player on the shortlist. In the end, the title went to a player three years his senior, Tottenham Hotspur's Kyle Walker. But it didn't matter. Alex's skill on the pitch had been officially recognized.

A Favourite with the Fans

It didn't take long for Arsenal supporters to take to their new player. They called him 'the Ox'. Two weeks after his arrival at the Emirates Stadium, Alex was featured in an interview in the club programme for the game against Swansea City. "There's no doubt that Arsenal have signed a gem," it declared.

Asked how he was settling in, Alex confirmed that the team had welcomed him. He already felt that Arsenal was his home. "Theo's helped me out a lot," he said, speaking of Theo Walcott, who six years earlier had also moved from Southampton to Arsenal. "I'm just trying my hardest in every training session and trying to improve as much as I can."

These words delighted every fan who read them. And their growing loyalty to Alex could be seen during the home match against Manchester United on 22 January 2012.

It was the first Premier League match Alex had started for Arsenal, and he was playing well. He contributed an assist to Robin van Persie's goal in the seventy-first minute. But then, three minutes later, with the score at 1–1, Arsène Wenger replaced him with Andrey Arshavin.

Before the match, Wenger had said it was important to get the balance right between giving Alex confidence and not putting too much pressure on him. But no one liked the decision to take the young midfielder off the pitch. The Arsenal fans booed loudly, and Van Persie, Arsenal's captain, was seen disagreeing with the manager. Arsenal went on to lose the match 2–1.

From that disappointing debut match against Manchester United to his nomination for Young Player of the Year award and acceptance by the fans, the 2011–2012 season was a rollercoaster. But for Alex himself, the highlight was when his boyhood idol, Thierry Henry, came to Arsenal – on loan from the New York Red Bulls – during January and February. "I was a bit starstruck at first," he admitted. "I think a lot of people were. When I went away with the England Under-21s, all these established players who play in the Premier League were asking me, 'What's Thierry like?'"

ON THE
EUROPEAN STAGE

The qualifying matches for UEFA Euro 2012 had
taken place over 2010–2011. The tournament was
set to be held in Poland and Ukraine between 8 June
and 1 July 2012. That year, sixteen finalist countries
attended, each one taking a squad of twenty-three
players. As the date approached, the clamour to
include Alex Oxlade-Chamberlain increased, though
Alex himself remained more realistic about his
chances. "It's hard enough for me to get in the team
at Arsenal, never mind thinking about the Euros," he
admitted. "One day I do want to play for England but
it's for someone else to decide when."

That 'someone' was Roy Hodgson who, after the sudden departure of Fabio Capello in February 2012, had become England's manager. Impressed by the eighteen-year-old's recent performance, Hodgson brought him on to the pitch in the seventy-second minute of a warm-up match against Norway. The date was 26 May 2012, the score went 1–0 to England, and Alex had played his debut in the senior England squad. A week later Alex started in a second friendly, this time against Belgium, which again ended in a 1–0 England win.

As the Euro finals approached, Roy Hodgson gave a rousing pre-match team talk. "We've got good alternatives if he tires and it doesn't work out but he deserves to start on what he's shown us." But Alex was determined not to let anyone down. As he told reporters when the manager first offered him a place on the team, "He said it was down to merit and I just have to prove him right."

UEFA Euros 2012

The first match England played was on 11 June against France, with Alex on the pitch from the start. It wasn't the best game of his career – he didn't see a lot of possession, and he received a yellow card for a foul on right-back Mathieu Debuchy. It was, however, a promising start. As captain Steven Gerrard confirmed afterwards, "Oxlade-Chamberlain showed tonight that he's good enough for this level. He's still got a lot of learning to do. But playing with experienced players, he'll get there."

The next match, played on 15 June, was against Sweden. England won 3–2, but Alex only came on in the ninetieth minute. Similarly, in the third game of the heats, playing Ukraine on 19 June, he substituted Wayne Rooney, who had scored the only goal of the match, in the eighty-seventh minute. England ended up at the top of their group and went into the quarter-finals, the first leg of the knockout phase of the competition. However, after a 0–0 game against Italy, England were beaten 4–2 in the penalty shootout. On 1 July, Spain beat Italy 4–0 in the final – but by this time, the England squad were already back home.

Kick it Out

For Alex and the rest of the team, one unacceptable feature of the Euro 2012 campaign was the problem of racism. It was affecting the game at every level.

The previous year, on 23 October, England and Chelsea captain John Terry was accused of racially abusing Queens Park Rangers defender Anton Ferdinand. In the end, he was found not guilty. At the time, though, the Football Association decided to remove Terry as England captain until the court case was over. Unhappy with that decision, manager Fabio Capello resigned.

Caretaker manager Stuart Pearce oversaw one match – an England 2–3 loss against Holland – before Roy Hodgson took over. His immediate job was to prepare the England team for the start of the tournament. As 8 June approached, several high-profile footballers drew attention to the problems that people of colour – fans and players alike – might face in Poland and Ukraine.

At the time, former England defender Sol Campbell expressed concerns on television. Then Theo Walcott's brother tweeted that he and his father would not be travelling to the Euros because of "possible racist attacks". The press reported that, due to "safety concerns", Alex's family would not be travelling to watch the eighteen-year-old play.

In a statement at the time, UEFA repeated that its "zero-tolerance to racism" was valid on and off the pitch, and that the referee had the power to stop or abandon a match should racist incidents occur. It was alarming, therefore, that seven years later in a qualifier for Euro 2020, little had changed. England players faced racist abuse from a section of the crowd in Bulgaria, with manager Gareth Southgate twice threatening to take his players off the pitch.

The final result of that match was 6–0 to England. Six arrests were made. The Bulgarian Football Union president, Borislav Mikhailov, resigned and UEFA threatened Bulgaria with points deductions or expulsion from future international matches. Certainly something must be done, and soon. No one should ever feel threatened because of their religious beliefs or the colour of their skin.

On Home Soil

Back in England, 2012–2013 was a low-key season for Alex. Now nineteen years old, he played thirty-four times for Arsenal but scored only twice, with a further three assists credited to him. His first goal came on 26 September. In the fifty-seventh minute of a League Cup home match against Coventry City that Arsenal won 6–1, he fired the ball home from twenty-five yards out. His second – and only Premier League goal of the season – came in a 7–3 home win against Newcastle United.

This lack of goals was, in part, because Alex was seldom on the pitch for the full ninety minutes. In sixteen matches he was only a substitute in nearly half of all the games he played. This was frustrating both for him and the Arsenal fans. Despite this, on 19 December, it was announced that Oxlade-Chamberlain had signed a new long-term contract with Arsenal.

As well as home matches, Alex had also moved on in the international scene. He was in England squads that played Moldova, Ukraine, San Marino, Poland, Ireland and Brazil. On 12 October 2012,

Alex scored his first senior international goal when England beat San Marino 5–0. On 22 March the following year, Alex scored again in the return match, which England won 8–0. Then, on 2 June 2013, in a friendly against Brazil organized to celebrate the official re-opening of the Maracanã stadium, he scored in the sixty-seventh minute. The match ended 2–2, and Roy Hodgson was first to compliment him: "Alex is lively. He added another dimension and scored a very good goal." Alex himself was no less delighted. "To be able to score at a venue like this against Brazil is amazing for me."

A PAINFUL START
TO THE SEASON

Six minutes into Arsenal's opening match of the 2013–2014 season against Aston Villa, Alex raced down the left side of the pitch with the ball before passing to Olivier Giroud, who scored. It was 1–0. Unfortunately, before the first half was out, Alex and Villa defender Antonio Luna had a nasty collision, leaving Alex with a serious knee injury. Arsenal went on to lose the home match 3–1. Alex's news was even worse.

The injury left him unable to play for the rest of the year. He missed out on Arsenal's crucial Champions League qualifier in Fenerbahçe the following week and England's remaining World Cup qualifiers against Poland and Montenegro. "Gutted I'm injured so early in the season," he tweeted. Despite this setback, his excellent play earlier in the year – both for Arsenal and England – meant that he was nominated for the 2013 Golden Boy award.

It was ironic that, after his lengthy recovery, the first match Alex played – subbed on to the pitch in the eighty-sixth minute – was also against Aston Villa. This time, Arsenal won 2–1. Two weeks later, on 2 February, Arsenal won again, beating Crystal Palace 2–0. Alex scored both goals.

It seemed as though he was completely over the injury. However, this was not the case. Alex was unaware of it at the time, but the damage done to his knee had made him move his body differently to compensate. As he put it, "Your balance can shift when that happens and you start loading more on one side than the other, and that's when the muscle problems creep in. It ended up in my groin."

This secondary injury caused Alex to miss the last three Premier League matches of the season. That was bad. Worse was the fact that on 17 May he was unable to play in the 2014 final of the FA Cup, which Arsenal won, beating Hull City 3–2. There was, though, another football campaign that Alex feared missing even more.

The World Cup 2014

Roy Hodgson included Alex in the young squad he took to Brazil for the twentieth FIFA World Cup, scheduled to run between 12 June and 13 July. The midfielder was enthusiastic and optimistic about England's chances. "We are going to the World Cup to do the business and win it."

On 4 June, England met Ecuador in Miami, USA, for a warm-up game. Playing for the first time since 20 April, Alex said that he felt "like a coiled spring", and certainly his game was energetic. But then, in the sixty-third minute of the game, following a hard tackle from Carlos Gruezo, he was substituted off. The FA later confirmed that the twenty-year-old had suffered a medial knee ligament injury.

"It is very disappointing for Alex and the team that he sustained an injury on Wednesday," Hodgson tweeted, adding that he was "undoubtedly our best player in the time he played."

Everyone hoped the injury would not rule him out of the World Cup itself. Alex was not, however, fit enough to play in the England versus Italy match on 14 June, which Italy won 2–1. He described himself waiting for the hospital results, wishing for good luck. "I sat in the scanner with the fingers crossed on both my hands for the whole twenty-five minutes." But it didn't work. The injury also ruled him out of the matches with Uruguay and Costa Rica. And on 20 June, following Costa Rica's shock 1–0 defeat of Italy, England too was out of the World Cup. After destroying the host team Brazil 7–1, Germany went on to beat Argentina 1–0 in the final, and win the cup for a record third time.

All's Well That Ends Well

On 10 August 2014 at Wembley Stadium, Alex came on halfway through the match to help Arsenal win the FA Community Shield. They beat Manchester City 3–0. He scored his first Premier League goal of the 2014–2015 season on 27 September in a 1–1 draw against Tottenham Hotspur. Then on 4 November, he scored again to put Arsenal 3–0 up against RSC Anderlecht in the UEFA Champions League, a match that ended 3–3.

On 25 February 2015 – having recovered from another groin injury that kept him out of the team for four weeks – Alex scored at home against Monaco. Unfortunately, by the time it came to the away return match on 17 March, Alex was once again out of action.

This latest injury came on 9 March during an FA Cup match against Manchester United that Arsenal won 2–1. Five minutes into the second half, he had to hobble off the pitch with a pulled hamstring. This and a torn muscle-fibre injury meant that he didn't play again until 24 May 2015, the last match day of the Premier League. He was brought on in the seventy-seventh minute of the West Brom match, which Arsenal won 4–1. Six days later, in the final of the FA Cup, he came on at the end of the game – with just enough time to set up Olivier Giroud, to make the final score 4–0. It gave Arsenal their record twelfth FA Cup win, and enabled them to retain the trophy for the second year running.

And who did they beat? Aston Villa. The team that had first triggered the series of injuries which had plagued his career for almost two years!

A YEAR OF UPS
AND DOWNS

Alex scored his first goal of the new season on 2 August 2015 in a 1–0 win against Chelsea in the Community Shield. On 29 August, Arsenal beat Newcastle 1–0 in a Premier League match. The single goal was logged as a fifty-second-minute own goal by Fabricio Coloccini, though it was Alex's shot that clipped the defender's heel and went in the net. Alex had played well throughout, and was made Man of the Match.

Alex's only league goal that season – and the first away goal he scored for Arsenal – was on 7 February, against Bournemouth in a 2–0 win. Internationally,

Alex was also making his mark. In the Euro 2016 qualifiers, he made an assist in the 6–0 England defeat of San Marino, and scored against Lithuania in England's 3–0 victory.

Sadly, the season was again spoiled by a series of injuries. During October and November, a thigh muscle rupture put him out of action for matches against Swansea and Spurs, for the UEFA Champions League against Bayern Munich, and for warm-up Euro 2016 matches against Spain and France. Then, on 23 February, he suffered a knee injury in a 2–0 home defeat by Barcelona in the Champions League. By the end of April he was passed fit to play, but then a second knee injury – which he got while training – prevented his return. Not only did Alex miss the final month of the Premier League season but his hopes of playing in Roy Hodgson's England squad for the 2016 European Championships were over.

The FA Cup

Set up in 1871, the FA Cup – or the Football Association Challenge Cup – is an annual knockout competition for English football teams, both professional and amateur.

The qualifying rounds of the 135th season took place on 15 August 2015, with 736 teams taking part. The final was held on 21 May 2016.

Of all the teams that have entered the FA Cup competition since it began, Arsenal has been the most successful, taking the title fourteen times. The big question was, could Arsenal win the FA Cup for a historic third year in a row?

Injured during the 2014 campaign, Alex had missed the final. In 2015 he had come on in the ninetieth minute and helped secure the victory. In 2016, then, his hopes were riding high. In the third round he played for the full ninety minutes in a 3–1 win over Sunderland. And he scored one of the goals in the fourth round win against Burnley, which ended 2–1.

In the fifth round draw against Hull, however, Alex was only brought on the pitch in the seventy-third minute. Then he injured his knee. It kept him out of both the replay and the sixth round match against Watford that followed. Arsenal lost that game 2–1, and were knocked out of the tournament. Manchester United went on to win the cup, beating Crystal Palace 2–1 at Wembley Stadium.

Alex could only hope that the 2016–2017 FA Cup campaign would be more successful for Arsenal – and for him.

Alex's Style of Play

Many things affect the way a footballer plays – height, strength, psychological make-up. In the case of Alex Oxlade-Chamberlain, the fact that he played so much rugby as a youth seems to have affected how he plays football now.

In rugby, forward passes are not allowed. An attacking player with the ball must carry the ball forwards towards the opposition posts as far as possible, then pass it back to a team member.

When a good rugby player receives a pass, they will instantly charge forwards without considering other passing options. Speed, agility and power are used to make as much ground as possible. It is only when their path to goal is completely blocked that they pass the ball on.

This is similar to how Alex plays football. When he receives the ball, he launches into an attacking forward drive, keeping the ball with him as he storms ahead into any open spaces. As Alex explained in an interview with *Arsenal Magazine*, he was someone "that got the ball, ran quickly and tried to stay out of the way of any contact."

As a footballer, Alex generally played in midfield. Arsène Wenger, though, tended to play him on the wing or even use him as a wing-back. This made full use of Alex's speed, but not those rugby-like elements to his game: taking on players hard and firing long-range shots at goal.

In the previous season with Arsenal, Alex had been out of action with injuries for fourteen of the thirty-eight Premier League matches. This was unfortunate, but unavoidable. However, of the remaining twenty-four matches, he was only on the pitch for a maximum of nineteen minutes in ten of the matches he played. As the 2016–2017 season approached, it was becoming clear that something would have to change.

READING THE SIGNS

A quick look down the list of Alex's stats for the 2016–2017 season shows that things improved. For a start, he went for almost the whole year without an injury, only picking up a hamstring problem in the final month of the season.

In the EFL Cup he scored against Nottingham Forest in the third round and scored both goals in the 2–0 win against Reading in the fourth round. But then in the quarter-finals, which saw Arsenal knocked out of the cup by Southampton, Alex was only subbed on to the pitch in the sixty-second minute.

Overall, the FA Cup was more successful. In the

fourth round, Alex's assist – a ball floated across to Danny Welbeck – created the second goal in a 5–0 victory over Southampton. In the semi-finals against Manchester City, playing as a wing-back, Alex provided eight excellent crosses, including the one that set up Nacho Monreal's equaliser. He was made Man of the Match for his efforts. Then Arsenal went on to beat Chelsea 2–1 in the exhilarating final, Arsène Wenger's seventh FA Cup trophy with Arsenal.

Following his team's triumphant victory, Wenger praised his players. "We had an outstanding performance from the first minute onwards. This team has suffered. They've united and responded. They showed strength and unity and played spectacular football today."

On the Bench

Wenger's concerns, both for the team and his own future, were understandable. In the first Premier League match of the 2016–2017 season, Arsenal played Liverpool. The match programme bigged Alex up, listing his achievements and pointing out that he was about to make his 150th appearance for the club. However, although Alex scored a goal, Arsenal lost 4–3.

Arsenal went on to win ten of the next fourteen games and draw four, pulling themselves up to second place in the table. But then they slipped back again, ending the season in fifth position. Arsène Wenger had managed the club since 1996, and now some fans wanted change.

Matters came to a head in the UEFA Champions League matches. Arsenal had reached the last-16 stage, with Alex's goal against Bulgarian team Ludogorets helping them to get there. Then they played Bayern Munich. Away, they lost 5–1. Back at the Emirates Stadium for the second leg, a large group of angry Arsenal supporters gathered outside demanding, "Wenger Out!" The result of the match – a second 5–1 defeat – did nothing to help his cause.

Alex did not agree with this criticism. From his point of view, Arsène Wenger was impressive both as a manager and off the pitch. "He's been brilliant for me in my career," he said, and went on to explain that, even though Wenger was certainly not the only one to blame when things went wrong, Alex was sure he would take responsibility for the problems. "Because that's what a great manager he is."

Despite his words of support, Alex's own position in the team was also uncertain. In December, Arsène Wenger insisted that he wanted Alex to stay at the club, explaining how Alex's career had been stopped many times by injuries. "He has had many, many setbacks, and I think it's the first season where he's had a consistency of presence."

But looking more carefully at this "consistency of presence", Alex only started in sixteen of the thirty-eight matches; he was on the bench for four matches; for another ten matches he was only on the pitch for a maximum of twenty minutes. In short, despite his words, Wenger was not making full use of Alex's football skills. And the young player was not happy.

"I do want to get more game time," Alex said. "There comes a time in your career where you have to re-evaluate things and think, is that going to be here or elsewhere?"

Headline Rumours

As the 2016 season continued, the news was full of stories that Alex might move from Arsenal. "LIVERPOOL CONSIDERING AMBITIOUS JANUARY TRANSFER BID FOR ARSENAL'S ALEX OXLADE-CHAMBERLAIN", the *Daily Telegraph* reported on 28 December 2016. But the following day, the *Liverpool Echo* disagreed. "KLOPP – OXLADE-CHAMBERLAIN TO LIVERPOOL? 'NONSENSE'".

By April, the story was back. "FOOTBALL TRANSFER RUMOURS: LIVERPOOL TO BUY £35M ALEX OXLADE-CHAMBERLAIN?" the *Guardian* asked. A week later, in the *Daily Telegraph*, came the Arsenal manager's response: "ARSENE WENGER TELLS ALEX OXLADE-CHAMBERLAIN TO STAY AT ARSENAL FOR THE NEXT 10 YEARS".

In May, Alex injured his hamstring and, at the same time, was reported to be unhappy that Arsenal had not offered him a new contract. "ALEX OXLADE-CHAMBERLAIN'S FUTURE AT ARSENAL THROWN INTO DOUBT AS WINGER GROWS FRUSTRATED WITH NEW DEAL DELAY", claimed the *Daily Mail* on 17 June. Suddenly everyone seemed interested in the young midfielder. "ALEX OXLADE-CHAMBERLAIN WANTED BY CHELSEA, LIVERPOOL AND MAN CITY", *Sky Sports News* reported on 19 June.

The headline rumours grew more extreme. "ARSENAL OFFER ALEX OXLADE CHAMBERLAIN £180,000 A WEEK – BUT CHELSEA CONFIDENT THEY CAN LURE ENGLAND MIDFIELDER TO STAMFORD BRIDGE", reported the *Daily Telegraph* on 24 August.

The new season began. Alex was still with Arsenal. Then, on 27 August, Arsenal were crushed by Liverpool. At 4–0, the result was even worse than the year before. It was a wake-up call for Alex.

"RED-HOT LIVERPOOL HAMMER HAPLESS GUNNERS", reported Ireland's *RTÉ* the next day. On the same day, along with all the other newspapers, the *Daily Telegraph* announced, "CHELSEA AGREE £35M FEE WITH ARSENAL FOR ALEX OXLADE-CHAMBERLAIN".

It wasn't true. And on 31 August, after several days of excited speculation, the truth was finally revealed. *BBC Sport* announced, "ALEX OXLADE-CHAMBERLAIN: LIVERPOOL SIGN ARSENAL MIDFIELDER FOR £35M."

Over his six seasons at the Emirates Stadium, Alex made 198 appearances for Arsenal, scoring twenty goals and helping them to FA Cup victory three times. Now, on the deadline day of the summer transfer window, Anfield became his new home.

A NEW START

"A new start is very often kind of a relief," Liverpool manager Jürgen Klopp commented. "You are in a situation with your old club – you are in a specific position, and accept it, and then at some point it's difficult to make the next step."

Alex had taken that next step. For a while, the press were sure he would go to Chelsea. But as he told reporters after his move to Liverpool, "I never thought about joining Chelsea." Liverpool, it seemed, was the only club he wanted to play for after deciding to leave Arsenal.

But why?

It was, as Klopp noted, much to do with the position he was told to play in at Arsenal. Time and again, Wenger had put him on the wing or used him as a wing-back. Klopp wanted to return Alex to midfield – the position that suited his style of play. "I grew up playing in central midfield and naturally I'm more of an inside midfielder," Alex pointed out.

A couple of TV pundits disagreed. On the day after the transfer Gary Neville – who had worked with Alex as England coach – said that although he would strengthen the Liverpool squad, "He doesn't get in the best XI". Then Thierry Henry, who had played alongside the young midfielder during that loan spell at Arsenal said, "I have been watching him for a very long time and I still don't know what he's good at."

Alex later admitted that he was aware of what they had said, adding, "I'm not here to make enemies. If that is what they think, fair enough." Although he was disappointed to hear those words coming from his childhood hero, there was nothing he could do if someone failed to recognize his strengths.

There were only two opinions that counted. His own: "Everyone says you have to be your own biggest fan and believe in yourself." And the opinion of Jürgen Klopp.

Number 21

Apart from his time in the Under-21 squad, Alex had worn the Arsenal number 15 shirt for the previous six years. At Liverpool, on 9 September 2017, he put on the number 21 shirt for his debut match against Manchester City. Alex was subbed on in the forty-fifth minute for what, unfortunately, turned out to be a 5–0 defeat for Liverpool.

Things could only get better. And they soon did.

Alex scored his first goal for the Reds in a 7–0 win over Slovenian club NK Maribor. The result was the largest away win ever by an English club in a European competition. In an interview afterwards, Alex talked about the game: "We were very clinical, and putting almost all of our chances away. It feels like we have a lot of goals in us, we create a lot of chances … and I'm ready whenever I get the opportunity."

On 4 November, in an away game against West Ham, Alex started for the first time – and scored in the fifty-sixth minute. And as the season progressed, Alex played more and more often. He made vital assists against Chelsea, Bournemouth (both home and away), West Ham, Newcastle and West Brom. He scored against Swansea and Manchester City. The latter goal – on 14 January in a 4–3 Liverpool home win – was particularly important as it helped break the Manchester team's unbeaten run.

In the Champions League, Alex punished Manchester City a second time, scoring from twenty yards out in a match that saw Liverpool win 3–0. Then, on 24 April 2018, having gone through to the next round, Alex suffered the terrible injury to his knee in the semi-final first-leg 5–2 victory against Roma. It put him out of action for the rest of the season – and a long time after that.

What had happened was a huge blow. Yet being unable to play because of an injury was perhaps less frustrating than being benched for financial reasons.

This, it was claimed, was what happened to him so many times during his six years with Arsenal. It all had to do with those 'add-ons' that in 2011 had added £3m to his fee when he moved from Southampton to Arsenal.

Add-ons

So what are add-ons? Let's try and make it simple.

BLUE TEAM: "We'll sell you the player you want for £150."

RED TEAM: "That's too much. He might not be that good. We might not even use him that often. How about £120?"

BLUE TEAM: "OK. But if you do use him a lot – like every week – you'll have to give us £30 extra."

RED TEAM: "I'll tell you what, we'll give you £15 if he plays more than twenty times in the season."

BLUE TEAM: "All right. Plus another £15 if he's on the pitch for the full game."

RED TEAM: "It's a deal. That's £120, with £30 in add-ons."

And that, according to Alan Gernon in his book *The Transfer Market*, is the sort of thing that happened with Alex Oxlade-Chamberlain. The main difference is that the two real football clubs were dealing in millions of pounds. Alex moved from Southampton to Arsenal for a fee of £12 million, with £3 million in add-ons.

What were the add-ons in this case?

Apparently, there was an unusual clause in Alex's contract. Arsenal would have to pay Southampton £10,000 every time he played for twenty minutes or more. This perhaps explains why he was used as a substitute so many times, often having to wait until the seventy-first minute before being sent on to the pitch. Finally, after his move from Arsenal to Liverpool in 2017, the length of time Alex played would be based on fitness and skill – nothing else!

Out of Action

Alex had been injured many times during his professional career. He had recovered well each time, but there was a cumulative effect. There often is. A pain 'here' can cause a problem 'there'; the damage to tendons and ligaments can have long-term effects. When Alex collided with Aleksandar Kolarov of Roma, it was not just the injury he got then – it was that injury plus all the other injuries added together. "An injury, within an injury, within an injury," is how Alex described it.

At first, he didn't realize how bad it was. Climbing to his feet, he tried to play on. But then he collapsed and was stretchered off the pitch. Newspapers reporting on the game suggested, "OXLADE-CHAMBERLAIN'S WORLD CUP DREAM IN BALANCE AFTER KNEE INJURY". But the situation was much, much worse. Not only did Alex miss the entire World Cup, but on 18 July, Liverpool confirmed that he would probably miss most of the 2018–2019 season.

"It feels like now is an appropriate time to tell people that for Ox, this coming season will be about focusing on recovery and rehab," Jürgen Klopp told the press.

The injury was bad. Surgery was necessary. After that, the long, slow journey back to match-fitness would begin. To help Alex return to play, physiotherapy was important. In addition, he would need support – from the team, from the coaches, from the fans, but also from himself. A player's mental strength is vital to achieve a full recovery.

"It all just hit me at once," Alex said, describing the horror of realizing exactly what had happened. "The day I found out the news about the injury I was choking up – but I am not that sort of person that feels down."

Alex clearly had the strength of character. Now it was up to his body to prove itself equally strong.

THE ROAD TO
RECOVERY

'Cruciate ligament rupture.' These are the medical words that described Alex's knee injury. No footballer ever wants to hear that this is the injury they have sustained. It usually means a recovery period of six to nine months – sometimes even longer.

There are four knee ligaments. One at the back, one at the front and one on each side. They are like rubber hands that attach the thigh bone (femur) to the shin bone (tibia), and prevent the knee joint from moving outside its normal position. If there is too much force to the joint, and the knee does move outside its normal position, the ligaments can overstretch and tear. With damage to all four ligaments, Alex's knee became very unstable, like a loose sail flapping in the wind.

There are two reasons why cruciate ligament injuries are common with footballers. First, because playing football involves lots of jumping, twisting and turning. Secondly, because of the physical contact during tackling.

Apart from Alex, many other top-notch players have also been put out of action by similar injuries. These include Zlatan Ibrahimović, Ruud van Nistelrooy, Paul Gascoigne, Roy Keane, Alex's two-time teammate Theo Walcott… It is a long list.

'You'll Never Walk Alone'

The surgery on Alex's knee took place eight days later, on 2 May 2018. It was the same day as Liverpool's return match against Roma. That game ended 4–2 to Roma, but Liverpool had won 7–6 on aggregate. They went on to play Real Madrid in the final, which they lost 3–1. There is no knowing what the result might have been if Alex had been able to play.

Jürgen Klopp, however, would not hurry his injured midfielder. "I cannot wait to have him back with us for matches," he said. "But we will wait for him and we will show the patience that is required to make sure he comes back ready to continue where he left off: as one of the most outstanding performers in European football."

Equally, Alex had always been impressed with Klopp as a manager and looked up to him. "Watching him, you see his passion and how much he cares about the game... The thing that stood out for me was his relationship with the players on and off the field."

The support from his manager, as well as from the rest of the team, was important for Alex. During his recovery, it was often just him and the medical staff, but Klopp's words of encouragement assured him that he was not alone.

As the months passed, he kept his many online followers informed about how it was all going, sharing positive comments like, "I'm making progress", "I'm in good spirits", "I just keep plugging away", "You just get into a routine and keep going, setting yourself little goals", "I passed the ball the other day, not very well, but that was massive for me to know that my knee can kick a ball".

His fans – both old and new – responded. They offered him sympathy and support which kept his spirits up and ensured that he remained motivated. And should he ever forget that he was not alone, there was also a special song to remind him.

The song 'You'll Never Walk Alone', written in 1945 by Rodgers and Hammerstein for the musical *Carousel*, was adopted by Liverpool fans as their football anthem, and has been sung at the start of every match they have played for the last fifty-five years.

> *"Walk on, walk on,*
> *With hope in your heart*
> *And you'll never walk alone."*

Nicknames

It is often a sign of a person's popularity that they are known by a nickname – something to do with their name, perhaps, or something that sums up their character. 'The Ox', or simply 'Ox', combines the two – a part of Alex's name, plus the strength and stubborn determination that the word 'ox' conjures up.

It wasn't always his nickname though. When Alex was younger, both at school and at Southampton Academy, he used to be known as 'Chambo'. It was only when he joined Arsenal that the Ox nickname took off. As Alex himself explained, "Before that I used to sort of hide the Oxlade name because everyone said it was too long – but my mum never used to like it being left out because that was her part of my surname."

"Feed the Ox, and he will score!" Arsenal fans chanted. Soon he was the Ox to England fans as well. And by the time Alex moved to Liverpool, the nickname had stuck. Jürgen Klopp often dropped the word 'the', referring to his new player as Ox. As for the Liverpool fans, they too called him Ox – although when they came up with one song for him, they did go back to his full name. Sung to the tune of 'Enola Gay', by Merseyside band Orchestral Manoeuvres in the Dark, it shows that Alex had been accepted.

"Jürgen said,
He's gonna play him in centre mid,
O-oh words can't describe
When he's running down the right-hand
*   side.*
His bird is fine,
She sings belters all the time
So we sing again,
For Oxlade-Chamberlain. . ."

Little Mix

Throughout his life, Alex has stressed the importance of those closest to him, both for his character and his career. His mother cheering from the sidelines. His uncle and brother's support. His father Mark's advice and coaching, which showed no favouritism because Alex was his son – "He's always been honest with me." Theo Walcott helping him to settle in "from the first day onwards" when he moved to Arsenal. Thierry Henry who, back in 2012, gave him "endless amounts of advice".

Then in February 2017, it was confirmed that there was another important person in Alex's life.

Perrie Edwards, one of the four singers in the band Little Mix, a British girl group formed in 2011 during *The X Factor*. After months of rumours about a possible relationship between the two of them, Perrie posted a photograph of her and Alex in front of the Eiffel Tower. Since then, they have moved into a house together – along with her cat, Jack.

With so many people to count on – family, girlfriend, manager and team, medical staff, football fans and online followers – Alex Oxlade-Chamberlain was never alone. Everyone played a vital role in his recovery. In addition, Alex's determination to play again as soon as possible never wavered.

Waiting for Alex's return to the team was especially difficult for manager Jürgen Klopp. Finally, though, the waiting was over. Just over one year after his injury, Alex made his return.

THE OX IS BACK

It had been difficult to predict exactly when Alex would start playing again. The newspapers, as always, were full of rumours – some positive, some negative. Then in December 2018, three days after Christmas, Jürgen Klopp reported that Alex's recovery was going even better than anyone had hoped.

"Best news, best news," he announced. "He started going on the pitch and from the first step he looked completely normal. He is obviously very happy and *we* are very happy about the improvement."

By February 2019, the chances of his return to the squad were less certain. He had been taking part in some light training, but it looked unlikely that he would be up for first-team selection for another two months. Then, on 4 March, it was announced that he would soon be making his comeback after all. Sure enough, on 8 March, Alex was on the pitch in a Premier League 2 match, away to Derby, as a part of Liverpool's Under-23 squad.

By this time, Alex was twenty-five years old. Yet he was allowed to play. There had been changes to the contest rules in 2016, when the upper age limit was raised from Under-21 to Under-23. In addition, each team was allowed to field a goalkeeper above this age limit, plus up to three more over-age players who were born after 1 January 1993. Alex was therefore eligible to take part.

Although scheduled to play for forty-five minutes, he was taken off four minutes before half-time. At first, it was feared that the knee injury might be the reason. Later it was revealed that it was a minor hamstring problem, but Liverpool had decided to take him off rather than risk a more serious injury. After the 3–1 victory to Liverpool, Alex was asked how he was feeling. His response – "Yeah, all good" – was the one that everybody was hoping for.

The Under-23s coach, Neil Critchley, praised Alex's attitude. "I've never met him before and you can see he is a bubbly, positive person. You could see he was enjoying playing again. And he brought a calmness and maturity to our play."

On Friday 26 April, Alex finally made his return to the senior squad, playing against Huddersfield. Liverpool won 5–0, a victory that put them back at the top of the Premier League table. Alex had replaced Daniel Sturridge in the seventy-third minute. He was only on the pitch for seventeen minutes, but he was back. It gave the whole team a boost of confidence. Klopp was happy: "It is really good news. He is back in the squad and that is cool. Really cool." He also joked about the length of time the player had been absent. "We had to think, when we wrote the names on the teamsheet today, what we call him. There are a lot of options: 'Alex', 'Ox', 'Chambo', whatever – it was that long ago since we [last] did it."

Easy Does It

'Alex', 'Ox', 'Chambo', it didn't matter. What was important was that Oxlade-Chamberlain was playing again. The return, though, was slow and careful. After all, no one wanted him to suffer another injury.

There were only two remaining matches of the Premier League season. Alex was included in the team, but remained on the bench against Newcastle and played for only two minutes in the match against Wolves. On 14 April, though, he was in the Under-23 squad again – this time for a full forty-five minutes – in a game that saw Liverpool thrash Leicester 6–0.

Over the summer, Alex played several times, gradually building up his fitness and strength. On 1 June, he was in the team for the final of the Champions League, although he did not play. Liverpool were playing Spurs at the Wanda Metropolitano Stadium, Madrid. They won 2–0, and became the first team ever to win the European Cup six times. It was Jürgen Klopp's first trophy since moving to Liverpool.

Throughout July, Liverpool played a series of pre-season friendlies against national and international teams. Alex started in six of them, and was substituted on for two. Then on 4 August, he was brought on to the pitch in the second half of the Community Shield final: Liverpool versus Manchester City.

The Football Association Community Shield – formerly known as the Charity Shield – is an English football match, played at Wembley Stadium between the champions of the previous Premier League season and the holders of the FA Cup. If a single team wins both then, in the Community Shield match, they play the team that came second in the Premier League.

This happened in 2019 when Manchester City won the double. Liverpool came second in the league, so the match was between Manchester City and Liverpool. At the final whistle, the score was 1–1, which meant a penalty shootout. Alex, who had been brought on in the seventy-ninth minute, scored a fantastic penalty, the ball hammering into the top corner of the net. In the end, though, with a tally of five penalties to four, Manchester City won the trophy.

The start of the new Premier League season was looming. Alex had a new number on his shirt – the familiar 15. But Jürgen Klopp was still cautious

about playing him too soon. As he kept saying, Ox –
and everyone else – would have to be patient.

On Friday 9 August, Liverpool played their
first match of the season, beating Norwich 4–1.
Alex was on the bench, but did not play. Then, five
days later, he did start a match, though not in the
Premier League.

The UEFA Super Cup

Founded in 1972, the UEFA Super Cup is an annual
match, contested by the winners of the Champions
League and the Europa League. In 2019, for the first
time in its history, it was an all-English competition,
with Liverpool (who beat Tottenham 2–0 in the
Champions League final) playing against Chelsea
(who beat Arsenal 4–1 in the Europa League final).
The match took place on Wednesday 14 August –
the eve of Alex's twenty-sixth birthday – in Turkey,
at Vodafone Park, Istanbul.

History was also made that night for a different
reason. Stéphanie Frappart from France became
the first woman to referee a major European men's
game. Alongside her were assistant referees Manuela

Nicolosi, also from France, and Michelle O'Neill from the Republic of Ireland.

It was a tough game, with the 2–2 full-time score leading to a penalty shootout to decide the outcome. Liverpool won this 5–4. As Jürgen Klopp said after the match, "It was a very difficult game for both teams. It was all about winning it, and we did that in the end." He then admitted that his decision to include Alex in the squad from the start of the match had been a mistake. "He can play much better than he did, but that's how it is, and after a long injury you have to find the rhythm."

Alex certainly hadn't played as well as he could. That would come. But the Super Cup winner's medal he woke up with the following morning was an excellent birthday present!

THE BEST IS YET TO COME

Back in England, Alex was soon playing more regularly. On 17 August 2019, Liverpool played against Alex's first club, Southampton, in a Premier League match. Perhaps learning from his mistake in Turkey, Klopp played Alex in midfield rather than on the wing, and was impressed with his performance. "To see him play almost the whole game at Southampton on Saturday was such a positive moment for all of us, especially him."

Five days later – on 22 August 2019 – Alex's contract with Liverpool was extended. He had already made forty-seven appearances and scored five goals for Liverpool. Now it was time to put all the injuries behind him and commit for four more years.

"I'm really, really excited," Alex said. "It's been in the pipeline for a little while, so it's nice to finally get it done and just extend my time here, which I am really looking forward to." Then, for the fans who had supported him so loyally during the year-long recovery, he added, "I can promise the supporters that I'll give them absolutely everything moving forwards."

Jürgen Klopp was no less pleased. "When I heard Ox had signed his new contract with us, I am sure my emotions were the same as every Liverpool fan hearing the news tonight – absolutely delighted. This is because an absolutely outstanding player and person has shown his belief and commitment to our project here."

Fit at last, and displaying the pace, power and fearless play he is famous for, Alex has gone from strength to strength since that signing. In the Premier League matches, he was brought off the bench earlier and earlier, before starting the match against Newcastle – a 3–1 victory – on 14

September. In other leagues his performance was even more impressive.

In the European Championships, England played Bulgaria at Wembley. The final score was 4–0, with Alex coming on to the pitch in the seventy-seventh minute. In the EFL Cup, on 25 September, he started in the match against MK Dons – a 2–0 victory to Liverpool. Then, in the Champions League, Alex really showed what he was made of.

On Wednesday 23 October, the first-leg match took place against the Belgian team Genk. Alex started on the pitch. In the second minute he scored with a low fizzer that hurtled into the net as the goalkeeper stood and watched. Then in the fifty-seventh minute he scored again. It was a spectacular goal, the shot fired in from outside the area. Liverpool went on to win the match 4–1. Jürgen Klopp was the first to praise his midfielder. "The goals were sensational and very important for us. Wonderful."

In the EFL Cup on 30 October, Liverpool were up against Arsenal. Alex's new team was playing his old team. The match turned out to be a 5–5 epic draw, and once again, Alex scored a superb goal. It happened in the second half. Liverpool were 4–2 down, their two goals having come from an Arsenal own goal and a penalty. Then, in the fifty-eighth minute, Alex took the ball from the opposition, spun round and hammered a thunderbolt 25-yarder past the keeper and into the net. Liverpool went on to win the match after a 5–4 penalty shootout.

Then, on 5 November, in the second leg of Champions League, Alex scored against Genk a second time, to help Liverpool to a 2–1 victory.

In a fortnight, Alex had scored four spectacular goals. On 8 November, he collected the Standard Chartered Player of the Month award, having been voted by Liverpool fans. It is typical Alex that he was still asking more of himself. "Quality-wise, I am not too happy with my performance, to be honest," he admitted. "I need to keep pushing myself… There's more to come from me."

This self-awareness and determination has been a part of Alex's make-up throughout his career, from those early days at Southampton, through the years at Arsenal, to his current place in the Liverpool squad. It is the reason he has come so far – and the reason he will continue to grow as a player.

Alex has achieved Player of the Month. The Year of the Ox is still to come.

Alex Oxlade-Chamberlain Timeline

15 August 1993   Alexander Mark David Oxlade-Chamberlain is born.

24 June 1998   Alex's brother, Christian Benjamin, is born.

2000   Alex joins Southampton Football Academy.

2 March 2010   Southampton manager Alan Pardew gives Alex his debut – he is sixteen years old.

10 August 2010   Alex makes his first competitive start, against AFC Bournemouth in the first round of the League Cup.

20 August 2010	Alex signs a three-year contract with Southampton.
30 August 2010	Southampton manager Alan Pardew is sacked.
4 September 2010	Alex makes his first League One start at home to Rochdale.
23 October 2010	Alex scores his first league goal against Oldham.
2 November 2010	Alex is named Man of the Match for the first time, in a match against Dagenham & Redbridge.
8 August 2011	Alex signs with Arsenal for £12 million, plus £3 million in add-ons.
28 August 2011	Alex makes his debut for Arsenal in a game against Manchester United. Arsenal lose the match 8–2.
20 September 2011	Alex scores his first goal for Arsenal, in a Carling Cup match against Shrewsbury Town.

28 September 2011	Alex scores the opening goal in his UEFA Champions League debut against Greek team Olympiacos.
22 January 2012	Alex makes his first Premier League start for Arsenal against Manchester United.
January– February 2012	Alex plays alongside his hero, Thierry Henry.
26 May 2012	Alex debuts in the senior England squad in a warm-up match against Norway.
8 June and 1 July 2012	UEFA Euros 2012, in Poland and Ukraine.
12 October 2012	Alex scores his first senior international goal in a match against San Marino.
19 December 2012	Alex signs a new long-term contract with Arsenal.

19 August 2013	Alex sustains an injury from a collision with Aston Villa defender Antonio Luna.
13 January 2014	Following his injury, Alex returns to the pitch to play against Aston Villa.
2 February 2014	Alex scores both goals in Arsenal's 2–0 defeat of Crystal Palace.
4 June 2014	Alex is injured during the England vs Ecuador warm-up game.
12 June–13 July 2014	The FIFA World Cup takes place, hosted by Brazil.
10 August 2014	The Arsenal team beats Manchester City to win the FA Community Shield.
24 May 2015	Alex returns from injury to play the last game of Premier League against West Bromwich Albion.

30 May 2015	Alex plays in the FA Cup final against Aston Villa, which Arsenal win.
2 August 2015	Alex scores his first goal of the 2015–2016 season in a 1–0 win against Chelsea in the Community Shield.
5 September 2015	Alex picks up his twenty-first England cap in the Euro 2016 qualifier against San Marino, which England win 6–0.
12 October 2015	Alex scores in the 3–0 England victory against Lithuania in a Euro 2016 qualifier.
28 January 2017	Alex returns from injury to make an assist in the 5–0 FA Cup win over Southampton.
February 2017	Perrie Edwards of Little Mix confirms that she and Alex are in a relationship.

15 February and 7 March 2017	Two UEFA Champions League matches against Bayern Munich end up 5–1 to the German squad.
23 April 2017	Alex is named Man of the Match in the FA Cup semi-final match against Manchester City.
27 May 2017	Arsenal beat Chelsea in the FA Cup final.
27 August 2017	Alex plays his last game for Arsenal, a 4–0 defeat by Liverpool.
31 August 2017	Alex signs with Liverpool for £35 million.
9 September 2017	Alex plays in his debut match against Manchester City. Liverpool are defeated 5–0.
17 October 2017	Alex scores his first goal for the Reds in a 7–0 win over Slovenian club NK Maribor.
4 November 2017	Alex starts in an away game against West Ham and scores.

4 April 2018	Alex scores against Manchester City in a Champions League match.
24 April 2018	Alex is seriously injured in the first-leg Champions League semi-final against Roma.
2 May 2018	Alex undergoes surgery on his knee.
14 June–15 July 2018	The FIFA World Cup takes place in Russia.
8 March 2019	Alex returns from injury in an Under-23 Premier League 2 match away to Derby.
26 April 2019	Alex plays in his first Premier League match since his injury, in a 5–0 win for Liverpool against Huddersfield.
1 June 2019	Alex is on the bench for the final of the Champions League against Tottenham Hotspur in Madrid.

14 August 2019	Liverpool beat Chelsea in the UEFA Super Cup in Turkey.
22 August 2019	Alex signs a new contract, committing to stay with Liverpool until 2023.
14 October 2019	Alex plays in the England team that beat Bulgaria 6–0 in the Euro 2020 qualifier.
23 October and 5 November 2019	Alex scores a total of three goals in Liverpool's two matches against Genk in the Champions League.
30 October 2019	Alex scores against Arsenal in the EFL Cup, which Liverpool win after a penalty shootout.
8 November 2019	Alex receives the Standard Chartered Player of the Month award for October.

10 November 2019	Sean Cox, the Liverpool supporter who ended up in hospital after the Liverpool vs Roma match in April 2018, where Alex was injured, returns to Anfield to see Liverpool beat Manchester City 3–1.
March 2020	In an agreement between the Football Association, the English Football League, the FA Women's Super League and FA Women's Championship, play in the Premier League and international games is suspended mid-season due to the coronavirus pandemic.
17 June 2020	Premier League football resumes, with a 3–0 win for Manchester City against Arsenal and a 0–0 draw between Aston Villa and Sheffield United.
26 June 2020	Liverpool are crowned Premier League winners after a 30-year wait.

22 July 2020   Liverpool receive the League Trophy after the final home match of the season, a 5–3 win for Liverpool against Chelsea. Alex scores the final goal of the match.

Alex's Clubs

Southampton

Club name: Southampton Football Club
Nickname: The Saints
Founded: 1885
Current manager: Ralph Hasenhüttl
Current league: Premier League
Crest: A white rose, a tree to represent the nearby New Forest, a scarf to represent the fans, and a football complete with a halo for the founding saints

Arsenal

Club name: Arsenal Football Club
Nickname: The Gunners
Founded: 1886
Current manager: Mikel Arteta
Current league: Premier League
Crest: A golden cannon

Liverpool

Club name: Liverpool Football Club
Nickname: The Reds
Founded: 1892
Current manager: Jürgen Klopp
Current league: Premier League
Crest: The liver bird, originally an eagle but now a cormorant, with the words "You'll never walk alone"

Alex's Mindset

Crucial to the success of a sportsperson is their attitude – or mindset. This term was coined by a top American psychologist, Dr Carol S Dweck. She believes that people can be divided into two groups. Those with a Growth Mindset and those with a Fixed Mindset. The characteristics of these two groups are quite different.

Growth Mindset:

1. I can learn anything I want to.
2. I want to develop and grow.
3. When I'm frustrated by something, I keep trying.
4. I like challenges.
5. I learn when people criticize me.
6. I am inspired by other people's success.

7. Everything that happens in my life comes as a result of my own effort and attitude.

Fixed Mindset:

1. I'm good at some things and bad at others.
2. I want to look good.
3. When I'm frustrated by something, I give up.
4. I don't like challenges.
5. I ignore it when people criticize me.
6. I feel threatened when other people are successful.
7. I am what I am and cannot be any different.

Throughout his life – learning to play football as a boy, improving as an adult, and dealing with his long list of injuries – Alex has always shown that he has a Growth Mindset. It has helped him to become the successful professional footballer he is today.

Despite his amazing talent and huge success, Alex has always remained grounded. Jürgen Klopp desribed him as, "One of the nicest guys you will meet." This is the one thing that has been said about Alex all his life. From the teacher working with him on the school play: "He was a really, really nice boy and completely comfortable even if the joke was on him," she said. "My daughter was also in his class and always says what a nice person he was." To Adam Richman, American actor, TV personality – and lifelong Spurs fan – who met him by chance at Twickenham when Alex was still with Arsenal. "As a diehard Tottenham supporter, it breaks my heart that Alex Oxlade-Chamberlain is such a nice guy…"

But perhaps the last word should go to his girlfriend, Perrie Edwards. How did she describe him? "Perfect."

Alex's Questions and Answers

Over the years, Alex has been asked a LOT of questions! Here are some of his answers.

1. *What makes you happy?*

   "Playing football!"

2. *If you could be a professional in any other sport, what would it be?*

   "Golf."

3. *Who's your favourite athlete who is not a footballer?*

   "Usain Bolt."

4. *What superpower would you like?*

   "To fly."

5. *Is it best to have one position on the pitch?*

   i. "It's important for any player to be versatile enough to be able to play in different positions."

   ii. "The needs of the team come first, so if you need to fill in at a different position, you'll be expected to do that."

   BUT

   iii. "In the long run, it's probably better to tie yourself down to one position and really become established in one area to be as good as you can in that position."

6. *Are managers always right?*

"All managers make decisions, and sometimes they are right – and sometimes people say they are wrong."

7. *What pre-match routine do you have?*

"I always listen to music, from in the hotel room, getting ready, right up until game time. Music gets me excited. It gets me happy."

8. *What was your most embarrassing football moment?*

"When [after Alex had committed a handball during an Arsenal vs Chelsea match in March 2014] Kieran Gibbs got sent off instead of me. I then went to the referee to try and tell him it was me – mistaken identity – but he didn't want to know. That was pretty embarrassing."

9. *How would your friends describe you in three words?*

"I like to think funny. Caring … and loyal."

10. *Who would you most like to meet/have met?*

"Nelson Mandela. Just for everything he did for humanity in general. Him and Bob Marley. They would be my two."

11. *What have been the highs and lows of your career?*

"The highest point was scoring against Brazil in the Maracanã. My injury was the worst."

12. *What is your biggest football ambition?*

"I'll give you a whole list. To become the best player I can be. To win as much as possible, to play for England as much as possible, and to win with England. And yeah, I want to win the Premier League. That's always been massive.

And the Champions League. And everything.
Let's just go and win!"

FOOTBALL LEGENDS

HARRY KANE

Be inspired by Football Legend, **Harry Kane**!

Discover the inspirational story of this top
player's journey from his early life in London
following in the footsteps of David Beckham
at school to his successes with Tottenham's
youth team and dream role as
England captain.

Packed with footie facts and match stats plus
Harry's career highlights.

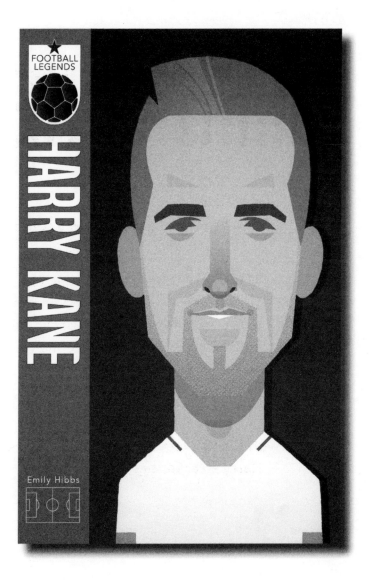

FOOTBALL
LEGENDS

HARRY KANE

Emily Hibbs

KANE'S
FIRST KICKS

Harry Edward Kane was born on 28 July 1993 at Whipps Cross Hospital, London, just five miles down the road from White Hart Lane, Tottenham Hotspur's home stadium. Harry's mum, Kim, was an assistant at a dental practice and his dad, Pat, owned a garage. Kim and Pat were loving and supportive, and Harry's big brother, Charlie, was his best friend growing up. The Kanes were a family of football fanatics and huge Spurs fans.

Almost as soon as he could walk, Harry was toddling down to the local park with Pat and Charlie for a kickabout. The small playing field wasn't exactly a world-class stadium. There were no nets or markings, and certainly no cheering crowds, but the trio made do with a patch of grass and a couple of trees for goalposts.

Harry quickly became as obsessed with football as the rest of his family, and a highlight of the week was going to see Spurs play at White Hart Lane. At his first match, four-year-old Harry sat in the crowd, proudly wearing his white-and-blue Spurs shirt, spellbound by the incredible players racing around the field below him. His favourite player, striker Teddy Sheringham, had just transferred to Manchester United. But as one of Tottenham's all-time highest goalscorers he was still Harry's hero, and his preferred footballer to copy at the park. After watching a match, Harry and Charlie practised the tricky tackles and skilful finishes they'd seen at the Lane.

A Sporting Start

When Harry was six the family moved to nearby Chingford, hometown of another legendary footballer, David Beckham. Harry dreamed of following in David's footsteps and becoming a sporting star himself, so when he spotted an advert for a trial at Ridgeway Rovers, the local club that David played for when he was a boy, Harry knew he had to go for it.

At the warm-up, the coach of Ridgeway Rovers, Dave Bricknell, introduced himself to the ten boys hoping to join his team and asked if anyone was up for having a go in goal. Harry preferred scoring goals to saving them, but he was keen to show the coach that he was happy to do anything, so he put his hand in the air to volunteer. Harry played well as a goalkeeper, making some skilful saves, and Dave was impressed. But then someone suggested that he should try Harry on the pitch – it turned out he was even better on the field than he was between the posts. Harry ran around the training ground, scoring goals from way down the field.

The trials were a success. Every week, Kim or Pat drove Harry to the nearby training ground, where he worked on improving his technique and building up his strength. He soon became Ridgeway Rovers' number-one striker.

Rubbing Shoulders with Rivals

Ridgeway Rovers had lots of strong players. Scouts from bigger clubs often came to watch their matches. Less than a year after Harry had joined the team, a scout invited him to a trial session for the youth academy of a Premier League club – it wasn't Harry's beloved Spurs, but their rivals, Arsenal! Still, the opportunity to play for such a strong team was too good to miss. Compared to Ridgeway Rovers' training ground, Arsenal's facilities were state-of-the art, with pristine pitches, gyms and meeting rooms.

Academy Trials

Big clubs like Arsenal and Tottenham Hotspur do not offer open trials. Instead, the clubs send out scouts, people whose job it is to search for talented players from local teams. Once a scout has spotted a player they think the club might be interested

> in, they make a recommendation, and the academy coaches might invite that player to a trial. At the trials, coaches look for players that can fill gaps in their current line-up, as well as someone with a strong technique and a personality that will fit in with the team.

Harry performed well at the trials and signed up with Arsenal for a whole season. He made the most of every opportunity, and though he wasn't as fast as some of the other boys, his powerful shots often found their mark. At the end of the season, however, there was bad news. On a walk to the park together, Pat put a hand on Harry's shoulder. "I've got to tell you something," he said. "Arsenal have released you." It meant that he wouldn't be continuing at the club. The coaches didn't think he was athletic enough and were worried about his pace.

Harry was disappointed. He'd done his best for the academy, even though his heart belonged to another club, and they had still decided to let him go.

But Pat wasn't fazed, he told Harry that if they worked hard, he'd be chosen to play for another club soon enough.

Embarrassing Photo

Years later, when Harry was playing for Tottenham, Arsenal fans found an old photo of him wearing the Gunners' kit at the academy and shared it on the internet. They thought the photo proved Harry wasn't a true Spurs fan. But Harry hit back at his critics, saying, "I wanted to wear a Tottenham kit but I don't think that would've gone down too well. I was eight years old … I just wanted to play football."

FOOTBALL LEGENDS

RAHEEM STERLING

Be inspired by Football Legend,
Raheem Sterling!

Discover the inspirational story of this young
player's journey from his early life in Jamaica
to life as a young immigrant in North West
London, where his incredible football talent
put him on the road to superstardom.

Packed with footie facts and match stats plus
Raheem's career highlights.

FOOTBALL
LEGENDS

RAHEEM STERLING

Musa
Okwonga

KINGSTON, JAMAICA, 1996

Raheem was just two years old, and he had only one parent left.

At the time his dad died, Raheem and his family were living in Kingston, the capital of Jamaica, in an area called Maverley. He was born there, six years after his sister, and it was the kind of place where everyone knew everyone, and where the children always played outside. When there was a storm, the rain would decorate the grey streets, and the children would rush laughing through the puddles; and because the rain was so warm, running in it felt like taking a shower.

People in Raheem's neighbourhood didn't have very much. They had to work hard just so there was enough for everyone. All they really had was their friends and their siblings and their mums and their dads, and some of them didn't even have that.

No one knew exactly what happened to Raheem's dad, but what they did know was that one day some people got very angry with him and went looking for him with their guns. When they found him, they didn't talk, they fired, and that's how they took Raheem's dad away.

It was one of the hardest times in Raheem's life, and it was about to get even harder. Soon his mum had to leave too. She couldn't find a job that paid well enough in Jamaica, so she went to the UK to study there and hopefully earn enough to support her children. Raheem was too young to understand why she had to go. All he knew was that he used to have two parents, and now it felt like he had none.

Surrounded By Love

But even though he had lost his dad forever and his mum had gone far away, Raheem was still surrounded by love. He and his sister went to live with their grandmother.

If he was good Raheem's grandmother would let him go and buy ice cream from the local shop. So many small towns in Jamaica have a shop like that, where it feels like you can buy anything. You normally find them on the corner of a street, and they look very small from the outside, but once you walk inside it's like being in a cave. You just have to tell the shopkeeper what you want, and he'll disappear into a little room at the back for a few seconds before coming out with whatever you asked for. You could ask him for some batteries, a toothbrush, a kettle, even a chicken – just give him a few minutes, and he would return with it in his hands.

That was how Raheem's life started: with some very sad times, but some very happy ones too. Ice cream, running through the rain – and, of course, lots of busy days playing football with his friends. But for him to have a life more exciting than he could imagine, he would have to get on a plane.

Coming soon!

Kick off your collection with more
Football Legends.

**Lionel Messi and Kylian Mbappé
available September 2021**